You'll smile and enjoy

Love

is ™ ❤ ❤

Real moments of showing Love to others.
Warm ~ Exciting ~ Funny ~ Meaningful
Perhaps you have some exciting Love is . . .
moments of your own.
(Please feel free to share a few with us.)

MW01167199

Thank You
Norm Caldwell • Taylor, MI
23649 Eureka Rd. • www.achievenowinstitute.co

**MY MOTHER'S
PUBLISHING HOUSE**

23649 Eureka Road • Taylor, MI 48180
Phone: (734) 287-2930
E-mail: norm@achievenowinstitute.com

ISBN 1-56273-246-3

Library of Congress Cataloging-in-Publication Data

PUBLISHED BY

My Mother's Publishing House
A Division of Achieve Now Institute

COVER AND GRAPHICS
Norm Caldwell

Why not write (or call), and let us know how much you
enjoyed our book. Toll Free: (877) 475-2525
*WE WILL TAILOR-MAKE LOVE IS . . . MOMENTS
FOR YOU OR YOUR ORGANIZATION.*

INTRODUCTION

Love is ❤❤❤

How would you share yours?

Hand one to a friend or lover,
include it in a card, letter, or gift.
Put it on a bulletin board or someone's desk.
Or 101 Love is ❤ ❤ ❤ *Bookmarks for you & yours.*

Love is Side Notes
make it easy to be THOUGHTFUL

YOU GIVE
IT AWAY
~ ~ YET ~ ~
YOU KEEP
IT!

Yours ❤ ❤

Give Away

IMAGINE THAT!

TWO
BOOKS
IN ONE!

CUT HERE

TWO
BOOKS
IN ONE!

PASS IT ALONG
PASS IT ALONG
PASS IT ALONG
PASS IT ALONG

Love is
Side
Notes

YOU GIVE
IT AWAY
~ ~ YET ~ ~
YOU KEEP
IT!

Love is ...

Treating each moment as though it has to last forever.

CUT HERE

Love is ...

Treating each moment as though it has to last forever.

My
Love is ♥ ♥ ♥

Love is™ ♥
♥
♥

Love is ... ♥ ♥

Friendship
caught on
Fire!

CUT HERE

Love is ♥ ♥
Friendship caught on Fire!

My
Love is ♥ ♥ ♥

Love is™ ♥
♥
♥

Love is ...

An understanding of each other's needs.

CUT HERE

Love is ...

An understanding of each other's needs.

My
Love is ♥ ♥ ♥

Love is™ ♥
♥
♥

Love is ...

Making your
house a home.

CUT HERE

Love is ❤ ❤
Making your house a home.

My
Love is ♥ ♥ ♥

Love is™ ♥ ♥ ♥

Love is ...

Rubbing their feet when they've been on them all day.

CUT HERE

Love is ...

Rubbing their feet when they've been on them all day.

My
Love is ❤ ❤ ❤

Love is ™ ❤
❤
❤

Love is ...

Taking responsibility for your actions.

CUT HERE

Love is ...

Taking responsibility for your actions.

My
Love is ♥ ♥ ♥

Love is™ ♥ ♥ ♥

Love is ...

Having dinner ready when they get home from work.

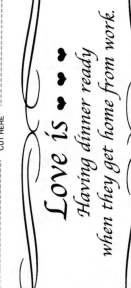

CUT HERE

Love is ...
Having dinner ready when they get home from work.

My
Love is ❤ ❤ ❤

Love is™ ❤
❤
❤

Love is ...

Hearing wedding bells
and knowing
they are for you.

CUT HERE

Love is •••

Hearing wedding bells and knowing
they are for you.

My
Love is ♥ ♥ ♥

Love is™ ♥
♥
♥

Love is ...

Taking the time to say

I LOVE YOU.

CUT HERE

Love is ... Taking the time to say I LOVE YOU.

My

Love is ❤ ❤ ❤

Love is ™ ❤

❤

❤

Love is ...

Being there
for each other.

CUT HERE

Love is ...

Being there for each other.

My
Love is ♥ ♥ ♥

Love is ♥ ♥ ♥ ™

Love is ... ♥♥♥

Taking the time to listen, instead of doing all the talking.

CUT HERE

Love is ... ♥♥♥

Taking the time to listen, instead of doing all the talking.

My
Love is ♥ ♥ ♥

Love is ♥
♥
♥

Love is ...

Bringing home something they have wanted.

(It doesn't have to be a special occasion!)

CUT HERE

Love is ...

Bringing home something they have wanted.

(It doesn't have to be a special occasion!)

My
Love is ♥ ♥ ♥

Love is ™ ♥
♥
♥

Love is ... ❤❤

Taking the time to take care of yourself as well as others.

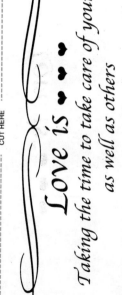

CUT HERE

Love is ... ❤❤

Taking the time to take care of yourself as well as others

My
Love is ♥ ♥ ♥

Love is™ ♥
♥
♥

Love is ... ♥ ♥ ♥

*Showing respect
to your other half.*

CUT HERE

Love is ... ♥ ♥ ♥

Showing respect to your other half.

My

Love is ♥ ♥ ♥

Love is ™ ♥

♥

♥

Love is ... ♥ ♥ ♥

Never going
to bed angry.

CUT HERE

Love is ... ♥ ♥ ♥
Never going to bed angry.

My
Love is ♥ ♥ ♥

Love is™ ♥ ♥ ♥

Love is ...

Opening the door when their hands are full.

CUT HERE

Love is ♥♥♥

Opening the door when their hands are full.

My

Love is ♥ ♥ ♥

Love is ™ ♥

♥

♥

Love is ... ♥♥

Picking up their
favorite snack
instead of yours.

CUT HERE

Love is ... ♥♥

Picking up their favorite snack
instead of yours.

My
Love is ♥ ♥ ♥

Love is™ ♥
♥
♥

Love is ... ♥ ♥

*Complimenting them
on how good they look
without being asked.*

Love is ... ♥ ♥

*Complimenting them on how good they look
without being asked.*

CUT HERE

My
Love is ♥ ♥ ♥

Love is ♥ ™
♥ ♥
♥

Love is ...

Waking up in the middle of the night when a loved one is sick and trying to help.

CUT HERE

Love is ...

Waking up in the middle of the night when a loved one is sick and trying to help.

My

Love is ♥ ♥ ♥

Love is™ ♥
♥ ♥
♥

Love is ... ♥ ♥ ♥

Buying them that

item that was

much too expensive.

CUT HERE

Love is ... ♥ ♥ ♥

Buying them that item that was much too expensive.

My
Love is ❤ ❤ ❤

Love is ™ ❤
❤
❤

Love is ...

Handing them the phone instead of dropping it on the counter.

CUT HERE

Love is ...

Handing them the phone instead of dropping it on the counter.

My
Love is ♥ ♥ ♥

Love is ♥ ♥ ♥ ™

Love is ... ♥♥♥

Changing your

plans too.

CUT HERE

Love is ♥♥♥
Changing your plans too.

My

Love is ♥ ♥ ♥

Love is™ ♥

♥

♥

Love is ...

*A hug or kiss
when you are leaving.*

Love is • • •

A hug or kiss when you are leaving.

CUT HERE

My
Love is ♥ ♥ ♥

Love is ™ ♥
♥
♥

Love is ...

Waving to them as you are driving away.

CUT HERE

Love is ...

Waving to them as you are driving away.

My

Love is ♥ ♥ ♥

Love is™ ♥
♥
♥

Love is ... ♥♥♥

Eating something that you don't particularly care for.

CUT HERE

Love is ♥♥♥

Eating something that you don't particularly care for.

My
Love is ♥ ♥ ♥

Love is™ ♥
♥
♥

Love is ...

Not continuing to talk on the phone when the family is waiting for you.

CUT HERE

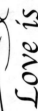

Love is ...

Not continuing to talk on the phone when the family is waiting for you.

My
Love is ❤ ❤ ❤

Love is ™ ❤
❤
❤

Love is ... ❤❤❤

Changing the oil every 3000 miles.

CUT HERE

Love is ...

Changing the oil every 3000 miles.

My

Love is ♥ ♥ ♥

Love is ™ ♥
♥
♥

Love is ... ♥♥

Saying I love you too when it is said to you.

CUT HERE

Love is ♥♥

Saying I love you too when it is said to you.

My
Love is ♥ ♥ ♥

Love is™ ♥
♥
♥

Love is ... ♥♥

Stopping when on vacation

to look at attractions

they might like.

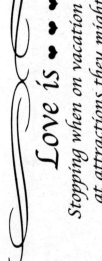

CUT HERE

Love is ... ♥♥

Stopping when on vacation to look at attractions they might like.

My
Love is ❤ ❤ ❤

Love is™ ❤ ❤ ❤

Love is ... ♥♥♥

Walking slower so they can keep up with you.

CUT HERE

Love is ... ♥♥♥

Walking slower so they can keep up with you.

My

Love is ❤ ❤ ❤

Love is™ ❤
❤
❤

Love is ... ♥♥♥

Going out of your way when their vehicle breaks down. (Super love is changing a flat tire in a downpour!)

CUT HERE

Love is ...

Going out of your way when their vehicle breaks down. (Super love is changing a flat tire in a downpour!)

My
Love is ♥ ♥ ♥

Love is™ ♥ ♥ ♥

Love is ...

Picking a night to go out every week, just the two of you.

CUT HERE

Love is ...

Picking a night to go out every week, just the two of you.

My
Love is ♥ ♥ ♥

Love is™ ♥ ♥ ♥

Love is ... ❤❤❤

Discussing a problem in private, not public.

CUT HERE

Love is ... ❤❤❤

Discussing a problem in private, not public.

My
Love is ♥ ♥ ♥

Love is™ ♥
♥
♥

Love is ... ♥♥♥

Showing mutual respect by hearing the other person out.

CUT HERE

Love is ... ♥♥♥

Showing mutual respect by hearing the other person out.

My

Love is ❤ ❤ ❤

Love is™ ❤ ❤ ❤

Love is ... ♥ ♥ ♥

Getting up in the middle of the night to check out a noise they heard.

CUT HERE

Love is ... ♥ ♥ ♥

Getting up in the middle of the night to check out a noise they heard.

My
Love is ♥ ♥ ♥

Love is™ ♥ ♥ ♥

Love is ...

Calling to say
you'll be late
for dinner.

CUT HERE

Love is ...
Calling to say you'll be late for dinner.

My
Love is ❤ ❤ ❤

Love is™ ❤
❤
❤

Love is ...

Filling up the gas tank to save them some time.

CUT HERE

Love is ...

Filling up the gas tank to save them some time.

My
Love is ♥ ♥ ♥

Love is™ ♥ ♥ ♥

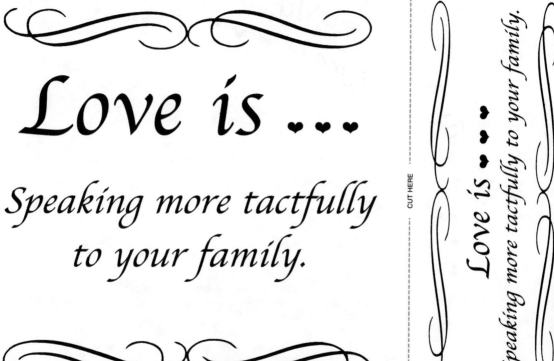

Love is ...

Speaking more tactfully to your family.

CUT HERE

Love is ...

Speaking more tactfully to your family.

My
Love is ♥ ♥ ♥

Love is™ ♥ ♥ ♥

Love is ... ♥ ♥ ♥

Keeping your mind open

no matter what is

being said.

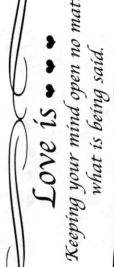

CUT HERE

Love is ... ♥ ♥ ♥

Keeping your mind open no matter what is being said.

My
Love is ♥ ♥ ♥

Love is™
♥
♥
♥

Love is ...

*Being able to
show emotions.*

CUT HERE

Love is ...

Being able to show emotions.

My
Love is ♥ ♥ ♥

Love is™ ♥ ♥ ♥

Love is ...

Playing with the kids after work, even though you are dead tired.

CUT HERE

Love is ...

Playing with the kids after work, even though you are dead tired.

My

Love is ❤ ❤ ❤

Love is ™ ❤ ❤ ❤

Love is ... ♥ ♥ ♥

Rubbing their back without being asked.

CUT HERE

Love is ♥ ♥ ♥
Rubbing their back without being asked.

My
Love is ❤ ❤ ❤

Love is ❤ ❤ ❤ ™

Love is ... ♥♥♥

Not always having to be the winner.

CUT HERE

Love is ♥♥♥

Not always having to be the winner.

My
Love is ❤ ❤ ❤

Love is™ ❤
❤
❤

Love is ...

Being there for them no matter what happens.

CUT HERE

Love is ...

Being there for them no matter what happens.

My
Love is ❤ ❤ ❤

Love is™ ❤ ❤ ❤

Love is ...

Cooking their favorite meal.

CUT HERE

Love is ...

Cooking their favorite meal.

My
Love is ❤ ❤ ❤

Love is™ ❤
❤
❤

Love is ... ♥♥♥

Wanting to spend time with them only.

CUT HERE

Love is ... ♥♥♥

Wanting to spend time with them only.

My
Love is ♥ ♥ ♥

Love is ♥
♥
♥

Love is ... ♥ ♥ ♥

Waiting in line to pay while they continue to look around.

CUT HERE

Love is • • •

Waiting in line to pay while they continue to look around.

My
Love is ♥ ♥ ♥

Love is™ ♥
♥
♥

Love is ...

*Watching them sleep,
knowing you are the
one in their thoughts.*

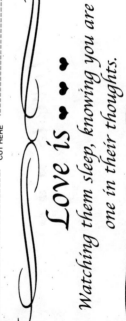

CUT HERE

Love is ...

*Watching them sleep, knowing you are the
one in their thoughts.*

My
Love is ♥ ♥ ♥

Love is™ ♥
♥
♥

Love is ...

Knowing what they are
going to say,
before they say it.

CUT HERE

Love is ...

Knowing what they are going to say,
before they say it.

My
Love is ♥ ♥ ♥

Love is™ ♥ ♥ ♥

Love is ... ♥ ♥ ♥

Sharing your concerns about what's going on with them.

CUT HERE

Love is ♥ ♥ ♥

Sharing your concerns about what's going on with them.

My
Love is ♥ ♥ ♥

Love is™ ♥ ♥ ♥

Love is ...

*Giving up the
remote control.*

CUT HERE

Love is ...

Giving up the remote control.

My
Love is ♥ ♥ ♥

Love is™ ♥ ♥ ♥

Love is ...

*Being nice to the in-laws
even though they tell
you that you're
doing it all wrong.*

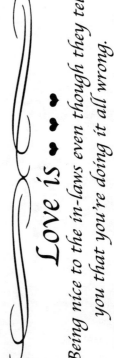

CUT HERE

Love is ...

*Being nice to the in-laws even though they tell
you that you're doing it all wrong.*

My
Love is ♥♥♥

Love is™ ♥♥♥

Love is ... ♥♥

Releasing your anger before it comes out in words.

CUT HERE

Love is ... ♥♥♥

Releasing your anger before it comes out in words.

My
Love is ♥ ♥ ♥

Love is™ ♥
♥
♥

Love is ...

Leaving work early,

just to surprise them

with dinner.

Love is ...

Leaving work early, just to surprise them with dinner.

CUT HERE

My
Love is ♥ ♥ ♥

Love is™ ♥ ♥ ♥

Love is ...

Holding their hand
as you watch TV.

CUT HERE

Love is ...
Holding their hand as you watch TV.

My
Love is ❤ ❤ ❤

Love is ™ ❤ ❤ ❤

Love is ... ♥♥♥

Watching sports, although you don't understand the game.

CUT HERE

Love is ...

Watching sports, although you don't understand the game.

My
Love is ♥ ♥ ♥

Love is™ ♥ ♥ ♥

Love is ... ♥♥♥

Running to the store at midnight to buy the ice cream they are craving.

CUT HERE

Love is ... ♥♥♥

Running to the store at midnight to buy the ice cream they are craving.

My
Love is ❤ ❤ ❤

Love is™ ❤
❤
❤ ❤

Love is ...

Standing up for the one you love.

CUT HERE

Love is ...

Standing up for the one you love.

My
Love is ❤ ❤ ❤

Love is™
❤
❤
❤

Love is ... ♥ ♥ ♥

Telling them your love continues to grow as the years go flying by.

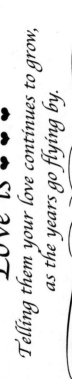

CUT HERE

Love is ... ♥ ♥ ♥

Telling them your love continues to grow, as the years go flying by.

My
Love is ♥ ♥ ♥

Love is ™ ♥ ♥ ♥

Love is ... ♥ ♥

Supporting the decision of them working long hours although you hate being alone.

CUT HERE

Love is ♥ ♥ ♥

Supporting the decision of them working long hours although you hate being alone.

My
Love is ♥ ♥ ♥

Love is ™ ♥ ♥ ♥

Love is ... ♥♥♥

Waking up early,
just to make them
breakfast in bed.

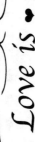

CUT HERE

Love is ... ♥♥♥
Waking up early, just to make
them breakfast in bed.

My
Love is ♥ ♥ ♥

Love is™ ♥ ♥ ♥

Love is ...

Doing the laundry when you see it needs to be done.

CUT HERE

Love is ...

Doing the laundry when you see it needs to be done.

My
Love is ♥ ♥ ♥

Love is™ ♥ ♥ ♥

Love is ...

Not questioning them when they come home late.

CUT HERE

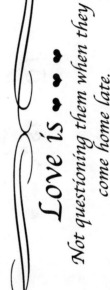

Love is ...

Not questioning them when they come home late.

My
Love is ❤ ❤ ❤

Love is™ ❤ ❤ ❤

Love is ...

Saying dinner was fine. (Even if it was a little burnt.)

CUT HERE

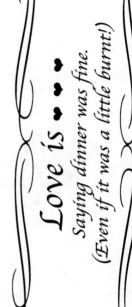

Love is ...

Saying dinner was fine. (Even if it was a little burnt!)

My
Love is ❤ ❤ ❤

Love is ❤ ❤ ❤ ™

Love is ...

Communication.

CUT HERE

Love is ❤❤❤
Communication.

My
Love is ♥ ♥ ♥

Love is ™ ♥
♥
♥

Love is ...

Letting the phone ring since the two of you are talking.

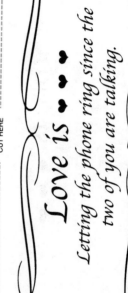

CUT HERE

Love is ...

Letting the phone ring since the two of you are talking.

My

Love is ♥ ♥ ♥

Love is™ ♥ ♥ ♥

Love is ... ♥♥♥

Looking into each other's eyes.

CUT HERE

Love is ♥♥♥
Looking into each other's eyes.

My
Love is ♥ ♥ ♥

Love is™ ♥ ♥ ♥

Love is ...

Us, not you . . .
not me . . . but US!

CUT HERE

Love is ♥♥♥
Us, not you . . . not me . . . but US!

My
Love is ♥ ♥ ♥

Love is™ ♥
♥
♥

Love is ... ❤❤

*Driving them
to their appointment
and waiting.*

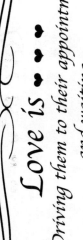

CUT HERE

Love is ❤❤

*Driving them to their appointment
and waiting.*

My
Love is ❤ ❤ ❤

Love is™ ❤ ❤ ❤

Love is ...

A nice hot bubble bath.
(With candles
surrounding the tub.)

CUT HERE

Love is ...
A nice hot bubble bath.
(With candles surrounding the tub.)

My
Love is ♥ ♥ ♥

Love is™ ♥
♥
♥

Love is ... ♥ ♥ ♥

Calling from work,
just to see how their
day is going.

Love is ... ♥ ♥ ♥

Calling from work, just to see
how their day is going.

CUT HERE

My
Love is ♥ ♥ ♥

Love is™ ♥ ♥ ♥

Love is ... ♥ ♥ ♥

Going for a long walk together after a hard day at work.

CUT HERE

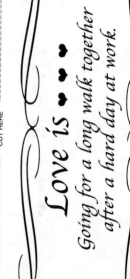

Love is ... ♥ ♥ ♥

Going for a long walk together after a hard day at work.

My
Love is ♥ ♥ ♥

Love is ™ ♥
♥
♥

Love is ...

Meeting them at the
door with flowers
and a bottle of wine.

CUT HERE

Love is ...

Meeting them at the door with flowers
and a bottle of wine.

My
Love is ♥ ♥ ♥

Love is™ ♥ ♥ ♥

Love is ... ♥♥♥

Leaving little notes for them to find, just to show you are thinking of them.

CUT HERE

Love is ... ♥♥♥

Leaving little notes for them to find, just to show you are thinking about them.

My
Love is ♥ ♥ ♥

Love is ™ ♥
♥
♥

Love is . . .

Slow dancing with no music playing.

CUT HERE

My
Love is ♥ ♥ ♥

Love is ™ ♥ ♥ ♥

Love is ...

Stopping the argument, even if you believe you were right.

CUT HERE

Love is ...

Stopping the argument, even if you believe you were right.

My
Love is ❤ ❤ ❤

Love is™ ❤
❤ ❤
❤ ❤

Love is ...

Losing track of time when in each other's arms.

CUT HERE

Love is ...

Losing track of time when in each other's arms.

My
Love is ♥ ♥ ♥

Love is™ ♥
♥
♥

Love is ... ♥♥♥

A soft kiss
good morning.

CUT HERE

Love is ... ♥♥♥
A soft kiss good morning.

My
Love is ❤ ❤ ❤

Love is ™ ❤ ❤ ❤

Love is ... ♥♥♥

Making love, anywhere, any time. (Even on the kitchen table!)

CUT HERE

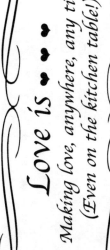

Love is ♥♥♥

Making love, anywhere, any time. (Even on the kitchen table!)

My
Love is ♥ ♥ ♥

Love is™ ♥ ♥ ♥

Love is ... ♥♥♥

Sharing your hopes and dreams with each other.

CUT HERE

Love is ... ♥♥♥

Sharing your hopes and dreams with each other.

My

Love is ❤ ❤ ❤

Love is™ ❤

❤

❤

Love is ... ♥♥♥

Renting a room
for a romantic
night out.

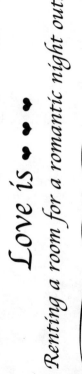

CUT HERE

Love is ♥♥♥

Renting a room for a romantic night out.

My
Love is ♥ ♥ ♥

Love is ™ ♥
♥
♥

Love is ...

Calling before leaving work to see if they need you to stop by the store.

CUT HERE

Love is ...

Calling before leaving work to see if they need you to stop by the store.

My
Love is ♥ ♥ ♥

Love is ™ ♥
♥
♥

Love is ... ♥♥♥

*Having coffee ready
when they get
out of bed.*

CUT HERE

Love is ... ♥♥♥

*Having coffee ready when they get
out of bed.*

My
Love is ❤ ❤ ❤

Love is ™ ❤ ❤ ❤

Love is ... ♥♥♥

Showing affection in public. (To a certain extent of course!)

Love is ... ♥♥♥

Showing affection in public. (To a certain extent of course!)

CUT HERE

My

Love is ❤ ❤ ❤

Love is ™ ❤ ❤ ❤

Love is ... ♥♥♥

Making love,
not just having sex.

CUT HERE

Love is ... ♥♥♥
Making love, not just having sex.

My

Love is ♥ ♥ ♥

Love is ™
♥
♥
♥

Love is ... ♥♥♥

Waking up with their scent on your pillow every morning.

CUT HERE

Love is ... ♥♥♥

Waking up with their scent on your pillow every morning.

My
Love is ❤ ❤ ❤

Love is™ ❤
❤
❤

Love is ...

Telling them that they are your dream come true.

CUT HERE

Love is ...
Telling them that they are your dream come true.

My

Love is ♥ ♥ ♥

Love is™ ♥

♥

♥

Love is ... ♥♥♥

Saying don't cook tonight, I am taking you to dinner.

CUT HERE

Love is ... ♥♥♥
Saying don't cook tonight,
I am taking you to dinner.

My
Love is ❤ ❤ ❤

Love is ™ ❤ ❤ ❤

Love is ... ♥♥

Asking how their day was before going into yours.

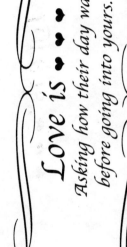

CUT HERE

Love is ♥♥♥

Asking how their day was before going into yours.

My

Love is ♥ ♥ ♥

Love is ™ ♥
♥
♥

Love is ...

Receiving your award and saying you couldn't have done it without them.

CUT HERE

Love is ...

Receiving your award and saying you couldn't have done it without them.

My

Love is ❤ ❤ ❤

Love is™ ❤ ❤ ❤

Love is ...

Making them smile or laugh.

CUT HERE

Love is ...
Making them smile or laugh.

My
Love is ❤ ❤ ❤

Love is ™ ❤
❤
❤

Love is ...

Not using up all the hot water in the shower.
(Shower together, it's more fun!)

CUT HERE

Love is ...
Not using up all the hot water in the shower.
(Shower together, it's more fun!)

My

Love is ♥ ♥ ♥

Love is™ ♥ ♥ ♥

Love is ... ❤ ❤ ❤

Remembering when your teen says I hate you, it's only their age.

Love is ... ❤ ❤
Remembering when your teen says I hate you, it's only their age.

My
Love is ❤ ❤ ❤

Love is™ ❤
❤
❤

Love is ... ♥ ♥

Not caring about the age lines on their face.

CUT HERE

Love is ♥ ♥ ♥

Not caring about the age lines on their face.

My
Love is ♥ ♥ ♥

Love is™ ♥ ♥ ♥

Love is ...

Seeing a rainbow after a personal storm.

CUT HERE

Love is ...

Seeing a rainbow after a personal storm.

My
Love is ❤ ❤ ❤

Love is ™ ❤ ❤ ❤

Love is . . . ♥ ♥

Letting them know you
would fly half way
around the world just
to be with them.

CUT HERE

Love is ♥ ♥ ♥

Letting them know you would fly half way
around the world just to be with them.

My
Love is ♥ ♥ ♥

Love is™ ♥ ♥ ♥

Love is ... ♥ ♥

Sending a limo
to pick them up
from work.

CUT HERE

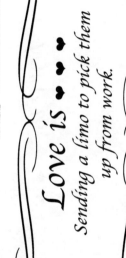

Love is ♥ ♥ ♥
Sending a limo to pick them
up from work.

My
Love is ♥ ♥ ♥

Love is™ ♥
♥ ♥
♥

Love is ...

Not running over the
cat when backing
out of the driveway.

CUT HERE

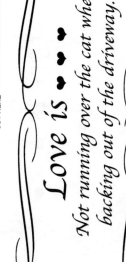

Love is ...

Not running over the cat when
backing out of the driveway.

My

Love is ♥ ♥ ♥

Love is™ ♥

♥

♥

Love is ... ♥♥♥

Being O.K. hugging your son as well as your daughter.

CUT HERE

Love is ... ♥♥

Being O.K. hugging your son as well as your daughter.

My

Love is ♥ ♥ ♥

Love is ™ ♥ ♥ ♥

Love is ...

*Feeling as good giving,
as you do receiving.*

CUT HERE

Love is ...

Feeling as good giving, as you do receiving.

My
Love is ♥ ♥ ♥

Love is ™ ♥
♥
♥

Love is ... ♥♥

All that and a bag

of chips!

CUT HERE

Love is ... ♥♥
All that and a bag of chips!

ABOUT THE AUTHOR

Norm Caldwell, Director
ACHIEVE NOW INSTITUTE

After successfully completing his tour of duty in the
military, Norm became interested in Psychology,
which sparked his interest in helping others and
ultimately led him to the study of the mind.
He attended the State Licensed Hypnotism
Training Institute of Los Angeles.

Norm's successfully proven techniques of Hypnotherapy
have helped thousands of clients reduce stress,
lose weight, stop smoking, and increase confidence.

As an author, teacher, and radio / television personality,
Norm has had the opportunity to touch the lives of
many people implementing meaningful improvements.
He has dedicated the last 18 years of his life to
helping people by sharing techniques that work!

YOU CAN TAKE CONTROL OF YOUR LIFE!

MY MOTHER'S
PUBLISHING HOUSE

23649 Eureka Road • Taylor, MI 48180
Phone: (734) 287-2930
E-mail: norm@achievenowinstitute.com

DYNAMIC SELF-ENRICHMENT AUDIO CASSETTES

BREAK AWAY SERIES

Break away from **SMOKING**

Break away from **STRESS!**

Break away from **FAT!**

IMPROVE your Concentration!

IMPROVE your Memory!

IMPROVE your Health!

Break away from **ALCOHOL!**

Break away from **DEPRESSION!**

Break away from **DRUGS!**

CUT HERE

BOOK PURCHASE SPECIAL

Thank you for your Purchase!
This COUPON entitles you to $2.00 off
EACH AUDIO TAPE ORDERED!
(Mail order only)

PLEASE PRINT

BOOK ORDER FORM

MY MOTHER'S PUBLISHING HOUSE

A Division of Achieve Now Institute

SHIP TO:

NAME: _____

ADDRESS: _____

CITY, STATE, ZIP: _____

PHONE: (_____) _____

CREDIT CARD INFORMATION	
CREDIT CARD NUMBER	
CREDIT CARD TYPE (VISA / MC)	EXPIRATION DATE
SIGNATURE	

SHIPPING

$2.00 - first book
$1.00 each additional book in the U.S.A.

Please allow 2-3 weeks for delivery.

Please send me _____ copies of
LUNCH BOX NOTES™
at $_____ a copy

Please sent me _____ copies of
Here's A Thought!™
at $_____ a copy

SUBTOTAL	
6% SALES TAX (MI RES)	
SHIPPING	
TOTAL	

MY MOTHER'S
PUBLISHING HOUSE

A Division of Achieve Now
23649 Eureka Road • Taylor, MI 48180
Phone: (734) 287-2930
www.achievenowinstitute.com

1 - 5 BOOKS for $7.95 ea.
6 - 25 BOOKS for $7.45 ea.
26 - 50 BOOKS for $6.95 ea.
51 - 100 BOOKS for $6.45 ea.

(CALL DIRECT for larger quantities)

PLEASE PRINT

BOOK ORDER FORM

MY MOTHER'S PUBLISHING HOUSE

A Division of Achieve Now Institute

SHIP TO:

NAME: _____

ADDRESS: _____

CITY, STATE, ZIP: _____

PHONE: (_____) _____

CREDIT CARD INFORMATION	
CREDIT CARD NUMBER	
CREDIT CARD TYPE (VISA / MC)	EXPIRATION DATE
SIGNATURE	

SHIPPING

$2.00 - first book
$1.00 each additional book in the U.S.A.

Please allow 2-3 weeks for delivery.

Please send me _____ copies of

Love is™ ❤ ❤ ❤

at $_____ a copy

SUBTOTAL	
6% SALES TAX (MI RES)	
SHIPPING	
TOTAL	

- - - CUT HERE - - -

MY MOTHER'S PUBLISHING HOUSE

23649 Eureka Road • Taylor, MI 48180
Toll Free: (877) 475-2525
www.achievenowinstitute.com

Make checks payable to:

1 - 5 BOOKS for $8.95 ea.
6 - 25 BOOKS for $8.45 ea.
26 - 50 BOOKS for $7.95 ea.
51 - 100 BOOKS for $7.45 ea.

MY MOTHER'S
PUBLISHING HOUSE

A Division of Achieve Now
23649 Eureka Road • Taylor, MI 48180
Phone: (734) 287-2930
www.achievenowinstitute.com

1 - 5 BOOKS for $8.95 ea.
6 - 25 BOOKS for $8.45 ea.
26 - 50 BOOKS for $7.95 ea.
51 - 100 BOOKS for $7.45 ea.

(CALL DIRECT for larger quantities)